BOOK
1

Composition Practice

THIRD EDITION

A Text for English Language Learners

Linda Lonon Blanton
University of New Orleans
New Orleans, Louisiana

HEINLE & HEINLE

THOMSON LEARNING

United States • Australia • Canada • Mexico • Singapore • Spain • United Kingdom

HEINLE & HEINLE
THOMSON LEARNING

Composition Practice, Book 1, Third Edition
Linda Lonon Blanton

Vice President, Editorial Director ESL/EFL: Nancy Leonhardt
Acquisitions Editor: Sherrise Roehr
Managing Editor: James W. Brown
Sr. Production Editor: Maryellen Killeen
Marketing Manager: Charlotte Sturdy
Sr. Manufacturing Coordinator: Mary Beth Hennebury
Composition: A Plus Publishing Services

Project Management: Anita Raducanu
Photo Research: Lisa LaFortune
Illustration: David Sullivan
Cover Design: Gina Petti, Rotunda Design
Text Design: Julia Gecha
Printer: Mazer Corporation

For permission to use material from this text or product contact us:
Tel   1-800-730-2214
Fax   1-800-730-2215
Web   www.thomsonrights.com

Library of Congress Cataloging-in-Publication Data
Blanton, Linda Lonon
   Composition practice
   Third ed. of: Elementary composition practice.
   p. cm.
   ISBN: 0-8384-1993-3
      1. English language—Textbooks for foreign speakers.
      2. English language—Composition and exercises.
      I. Blanton, Linda Lonon. Elementary composition
   practice. II. Title.
PE1128.B588   2001
428.2′4–dc21   01-179760

International Division List

ASIA (excluding India)
Thomson Learning
60 Albert Street #15-01
Albert Complex
Singapore 189969

AUSTRALIA/NEW ZEALAND
Nelson/Thomson Learning
102 Dodds Street
South Melbourne
Victoria 3205 Australia

CANADA
Nelson/Thomson Learning
1120 Birchmount Road
Scarborough, Ontario
Canada M1K 5G4

LATIN AMERICA
Thomson Learning
Seneca, 53
Colonia Polanco
11560 México D.F. México

SPAIN
Thomson Learning
Calle Magallanes, 25
28015-Madrid
España

UK/EUROPE/MIDDLE EAST
Thomson Learning
Berkshire House
168-173 High Holborn
London, WC1V 7AA, United Kingdom

Photo Credits:
7, © Tim Barnwell/Stock Boston; 17, © David Stoecklein/The Stock Market; 27, © Philip Gould/CORBIS;
37, © Palmer/Kane/The Stock Market; 45, © Roger Ball, The Stock Market; 53, © Bob Daemmrich/Stock Boston;
63, © Tom Wurl/Stock Boston; 73, © Tom Stewart/The Stock Market; 83, © Lee Snider/CORBIS;
91, © Richard Glover, Escoscene/CORBIS

Preface

This third edition of *Composition Practice, Book 1,* celebrates the continuing successful use of the series by many thousands of English learners. This edition should prove helpful for students who need practice in the kinds of writing found on state standardized tests. The basic instructional design and pedagogy remain the same, but several new features have been incorporated in response to user suggestions.

A pre-reading activity has been included in each unit, and post-reading caption-writing exercises are integrated with the all-new illustrations. An optional open-ended activity, *Connecting,* encourages students to develop computer skills by searching the internet for information related to unit themes. Additionally, the grammar progression is slightly accelerated in that it now includes the *going to* future as well as the simple future *will.* An appendix of irregular verb forms supplements the final unit, which introduces the simple past tense. An index allows teachers to locate skills found in state standards and on tests.

Book 1 is divided into ten units. Each unit contains an illustrated reading passage, followed by exercises on comprehension, grammar, vocabulary, semantic organization, and/or writing mechanics. An illustrated model composition—which makes use of the vocabulary, grammar, and organization of the reading passage—follows the exercises. Students are then presented with detailed instructions for writing their own compositions. All reading passages and models focus on certain purposes for writing, such as narrating and describing, and certain means of organizing ideas, such as chronological and spatial ordering. The assumptions here are that there is more to composing, on even an elementary level than mere sentence-level exercises, and that ESOL students can understand and use sophisticated principles and techniques of English composition writing without waiting until they are more fully fluent in English.

I wish to acknowledge my former colleagues of the English Language Institute at Central YMCA Community College in Chicago. With them I began the work that led to the *Composition Practice* series. Although the school no longer exists, it was an exciting place and time to teach and learn. I would like to give special thanks to my dear friend Linda Hillman, who had faith early on that a textbook or two could emerge from my jumble of mimeographed lessons.

I would also like to thank the reviewers, many of whose helpful suggestions were incorporated into this third edition:

Carol Antunano, *English Center,* Miami, FL

Nancy Boyer, *Golden West College,* Huntington Beach, CA

Miguel A. Contreras, *English Language Institute at El Paso* and *El Paso Community College,* El Paso, TX

Jeff DiUglio, *Boston University,* Boston, MA

Terry Paglia, *Newtown High School,* Elmhurst, NY

Kathleen Yearick, *Groves-Wilmington High School,* Wilmington, DE

Contents

UNIT 1 ● Introducing Yourself   1

Composition Focus: Narration
Organizational Focus: Expansion
Grammatical Focus: Simple Present Tense *(be)*

UNIT 2 ● Identifying Family and Home   9

Composition Focus: Narration and Description
Organizational Focus: Division
Grammatical Focus: Simple Present Tense (all verbs), *There is/are*

To the Teacher

It is commonly said that students learn to read and write by reading and writing. While the adage is true, its simplicity belies a complex process of development. This process is complicated enough in a reader-writer's first language and all the more challenging in another language. *Composition Practice* is based on many years of experience in mentoring English learners through the process of reading and writing, in large part by creating for them an awareness of rhetorical possibilities, providing clear direction, guiding their practice, and giving positive and useful feedback.

● **Who can use *Book 1*?** It is designed for adult students of English on an elementary level of proficiency. It is intended for people who are learning English for professional, academic, and business reasons. The lessons were successfully tested with students ranging in ages from 15 to 55, who—in total—spoke nine different languages and had educational backgrounds ranging from ninth grade to university degrees. Altogether the lessons provide about 50 class hours of instruction (roughly an intensive 8- to 10-week course).

● **How is *Book 1* organized?** It is divided into ten units, each containing a reading passage, follow-up exercises, a composition to model, and instructions for students' own writing. The readings progress in grammatical complexity in this order: from present *be* to *there is/are,* to simple present forms of other verbs and the present progressive tense, and then finally to *going to* future, simple future *will,* and the simple past tense. Many grammar books present English structure in this order, and students will probably be studying grammar and working on reading-writing simultaneously. The model composition in each unit makes use of the same grammar, vocabulary, and organization as the reading passage.

● **What is the textual focus?** All of the reading passages and model compositions in *Book 1* focus on people like any of us who work, play, study, and live our lives. This is a way to make the content realistic. Collectively, the texts tell the story of a fictional Italian family, the Baronis. Places in New Orleans are commonly mentioned—and most are real—but knowledge of the locale is not necessary for comprehension. Your students will substitute their own neighborhoods and familiar places in their writing.

● **What writing assignments do I give?** Instructions for student writing appear at the end of each unit with explicit directions. You and your students will need to go over the instructions together. In some cases, they may require your interpretation and explanation. After all, you will know what your students can handle—and what will confuse them. As students start their writing, closely supervise and you will see if they understand what to do by the way they are following through.

● **How do I use the picture sequence in each unit?** The visuals in each unit should be used for oral practice and writing. You will probably want students to follow the pictures while you read the corresponding text. Then students can narrate the story according to the pictures. Students will also connect words to pictures by writing captions underneath.

● **What rhetorical rationale governs** *Book 1*? All readings and writing models in *Book 1* are descriptive and/or narrative in purpose. These two rhetorical functions usually lend themselves to fairly simple yet authentic writing, and so provide an appropriate place for English learners to begin. The only texts that differ stylistically from the others are in Units 7 and 8, where the tone is more conversational because of a personal letter format. Students can become consciously aware of many fairly commonplace features of English writing as they progress through the materials in *Book 1.* With them, you will want to look at the diagrams in each unit as visual representations of useful organizational concepts.

● **How much time will the lessons take?** Each unit is designed to provide material for five hours of class work. If your students meet for composition five days a week, all the work can be done in class. If they meet for less time, the exercises can be done as homework, and you can still complete a unit a week.

● **How do I pace the materials?** The following is a five-day suggested breakdown of each unit.

DAY 1: Reading
Introduce the context of the reading by involving students in the pre-reading activity, *Before You Read.* Some pre-reading activities lend themselves to group discussion; others to pair or group work. Move then to the actual reading passage, but have students listen first with their books closed as you "tell" the reading once or twice. Next, have students follow along silently, this time with their books open, as you slowly read the text aloud. At this point, explain new words and grammar that you think will pose stumbling blocks. Now, have students read silently again—this time on their own, but with dictionaries in hand. There may be words they want to check on. Once they seem satisfied with their reading, ask questions that can be answered directly from the reading. It's fine if students actually find a sentence or phrase that contains the answer to a question and read it aloud. To allow further processing of new words and phrases, write sequential questions on the board and give students a chance to take turns answering without reading from the text. Finally,

turn to the sequential pictures and have students write captions for each one. This aids memory and helps connect meaning and image. At this point, using the pictures as memory prompts, some students may be able to (re) tell the complete story to the class.

DAY 2: Review and exercises

Use the pictures to refresh everyone's memory of the story and then have students complete the exercises, with the story as content for further language-learning work. If possible, have students work in pairs or small groups. If there is enough time, check students' answers orally.

DAY 3: Presenting the model for writing

If the exercises weren't checked before, check them now. However, be sure to have the model for writing be the day's focus. Present the model by following some or all of the steps used in presenting the reading on Day 1. After you and the students work through the model, go over the instructions for their (next day) writing. Work with students to help them start planning their writing for the next day, so their ideas can "percolate" overnight. Creating an outline may help; you may need to show them how to do this. Make sure, however, that students understand that outlining is a way to trigger thinking and start planning, not a rigid commitment. As they think, and particularly when they start writing the next day, new ideas may surface.

DAY 4: Writing

Have students write their compositions in class. It's fine if they use outlines or notes and even check the model periodically to "borrow" a word or phrase. Encourage them, however, not to simply copy. They will want to make their compositions their own, with as much of their own content as possible.

DAY 5: Wrapping up the unit

Finish up any work left over from Days 1–4. If you have read over their compositions, talk about common problems or needs. A mini-lesson on grammar or organization may be in order. However you give feedback or attend to common needs, always avoid putting anyone on the spot, except, of course, to hold up a student's work as a positive example. Based on your feedback, students might redraft, correct, or expand their writing. If your students have access to computers, you'll want to "close" out a lesson with the computer activity, *Connecting*, at the end of each unit.

If your composition class meets for fewer than five days a week, you may take as long as two weeks to complete a unit and still cover most of the material in *Book 1*. The schedule might then work like this:

DAY 1/WEEK 1: Reading

Present the content of the reading according to the steps outlined for Day 1 of the five-day plan (above). Students' homework for Day 2 is to do the exercises.

DAY 2/WEEK 1: Presenting the model for writing

Check homework in class by having students take turns giving their answers. Do this as quickly as possible in order to focus on the model and on preparing students for their own writing by going over the instructions in the unit. In presenting the model, follow some or all of the steps followed in presenting the reading on Day 1. Students' homework assignment is planning their compositions in outline or note form.

DAY 1/WEEK 2: Writing

Go over the model again to review, and quickly check on students' outlines/notes by having them briefly explain their plans. Remind them that their plans may change as they write and that they should be open to new ideas that may emerge. Students write their compositions in class while you circulate and offer assistance where needed.

DAY 2/WEEK 2: Wrapping up the Unit

Follow the procedure outlined in Day 5 of the five-day plan.

● **What is of ultimate importance if I can't do it all?** No matter what your schedule is, or even the limitations of your teaching situation, have your students do their writing in class where you can serve as a resource. The help that you provide them *while* they are writing is almost always more useful for their writing development than feedback on their papers *after* they've finished writing. When you do provide line-by-line feedback, try to do it in the context of individualized teacher-student conferences. A student then has a chance to ask questions, clarify your feedback, and feel more secure about correction.

● **What are the ultimate goals for *Book 1*?** By the time students finish Unit 10, they should be able to write a short (1–2 page) descriptive and/or narrative essay on a familiar, everyday subject. A competent reader of the essay should be able to perceive an introduction to the topic, the development of related and relevant content, and a conclusion. The content of the essay should flow in a way that makes sense to a competent reader of English.

To the Student

You will need the following materials:

1. a loose-leaf notebook

2. 8 1/2 x 11 inch loose-leaf notebook paper

3. a pen and pencil

4. a good translation dictionary and a simplified English-English dictionary

You should follow these rules for good reading:

1. Look at the complete reading selection before you use your dictionary.

2. Let your eyes catch groups of words; do not stop after every word.

3. Do not move your mouth when you read; read with your eyes.

4. After you read the complete selection, use your dictionary to find the words you do not know.

5. Read the selection again; look for important connections: and, because, after, before, while, etc.

You should follow these rules for good writing:

1. Leave margins.

2. Indent each paragraph.

3. Put a period at the end of each sentence; put a question mark at the end of each question.

   Example: John is absent today.
   Is he sick?

4. Use capital letters correctly:
   a. names of people
      Example: Peter Andres
   b. names of cities
      Example: Paris
   c. names of countries
      Example: Japan
   d. names of rivers
      Example: the Amazon River

e. names of streets
    Example: Michigan Avenue

f. names of buildings
    Example: the Empire State Building

g. names of organizations
    Example: the United Nations

h. names of national, ethnic, and racial groups
    Example: French, Jewish, African Americans

i. titles
    Example: Dr. Santini

j. the first person singular pronoun: I

k. days of the week
    Example: Thursday

l. months of the year
    Example: April

m. holidays
    Example: Christmas

n. titles of books, magazines, newspapers
    Example: the New York Times

o. the first letter at the beginning of each sentence and question
    Example: Are you happy?

Placement of Parts of a Composition

Your Name
Course

Title of your composition

[ ] XXXXXXXXXXXXXXXXXXXXXXXXXXXXXXX
XXXXXXXXXXXXXXXXXXXXXXXXXXXXXXXXXXXXXXX.
XXXXXXXXXXXXXXXXXXXXXXXXXXXXXXXXXXXX
XXXXXXX.
[ ] XXXXXXXXXXXXXXXXXXXXXXXXXXXXXX.
XXXXXXXXXXXXXXXXXXXXXXXXXXXXXXXXXXXXX.
XXXXXXXXXXXXXXXXXXXXXXXXXXXXXXXXXXXXX.
XXXXXXXXXXXXXXXXXXXXXXXXXXXXXXXXXXXXXXX
XXXX XXXXXXXXXXXXX. XXXXXXXXXXXXXXXXXXXX
XXXXXXXXXXXXX. XXXXXXXXXXXXXXXXXXXXXXXX
XXXXXXXXXXXXXXXXXXXXXXXXXXXX.
[ ] XXXXXXXXXXXXXXXXXXXXXXXXX. XXXXXXXX
XXXXXXXXXXXXXXXXXXXXXXXXXXXXXXXXXXXX.
XXXXXXXXXXXXXXXXXXXXXXXXXX.

[ ] indentation

left margin

right margin

Introducing Yourself

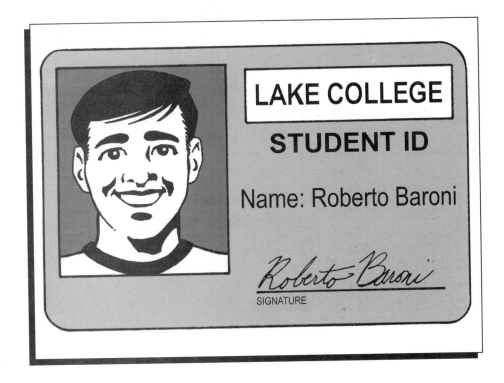

LAKE COLLEGE
STUDENT ID
Name: Roberto Baroni
Roberto Baroni
SIGNATURE

🌂 **Composition Focus: Narration**

🌂 **Organizational Focus: Expansion**

🌂 **Grammatical Focus: Simple Present Tense** *(be)*

1. _____

2. _____

3. _____

4. _____

5. _____

6. _____

7. _____

Reading 1

Before You Read

Think about this. Then talk about it with a partner or group.

Can you find these people, places, and things in the pictures on page 2?

student   desk

teacher   board

classroom   building

English

Can you find the country of Italy on a map or globe?

Read

Roberto Baroni

Roberto Baroni is a student. He is from Italy. He is twenty-one years old. He studies English every day. Mr. Peters is his teacher. Mr. Peters is a good teacher. He is kind and patient. Roberto and Mr. Peters are in the classroom now. They are busy. Mr. Peters is at the board. Roberto is at his desk. Roberto likes his classroom. It is a small room. It is clean and pleasant. The classroom is in a large building.

After You Read

Caption Writing: Please write a sentence from the reading under each picture on page 2, or in your notebook.

Exercise A: Simple Present Tense/Comprehension

Please answer the questions in complete sentences.

Example: Is Roberto a student?
Yes, he is a student.

1. Is Mr. Peters a good teacher?

   _____

2. Are Roberto and Mr. Peters in the classroom now?

   _____

3. Are they busy?

   _____

4. Is Roberto at the board?

   _____

5. Is Mr. Peters near the window?

   _____

6. Is the classroom in a small building?

   _____

7. Is it a small room?

   _____

8. Where is Roberto from?

   _____

9. How old is Roberto?

   _____

10. Where are Roberto and Mr. Peters now?

    _____

Exercise B: Simple Present Tense

Please write *is* or *are* in the empty spaces.

Roberto Baroni _____ a student. He _____ from Italy.
He _____ twenty-one years old. He studies English every day.
Mr. Peters _____ his teacher. Mr. Peters _____ a good teacher.
He _____ kind and patient. Roberto and Mr. Peters _____ in
the classroom now. They _____ busy. Mr. Peters _____ at the
board. Roberto _____ at his desk. The classroom _____ in a
large building. It _____ a small room. It _____ clean and
pleasant. Roberto likes the classroom.

Exercise C: Vocabulary

Please choose a word for each blank from the list below.

desk   teacher   building   classroom   English   student   board

1. Roberto is a _____.
2. He studies _____ every day.
3. Mr. Peters is a _____.
4. Roberto and Mr. Peters are in the _____ now.
5. Mr. Peters is at the _____.
6. Roberto is at his _____.
7. The classroom is in a large _____.

Exercise D: Simple Present Tense/ Interrogative Form

Please change the statements to questions. Write the questions in your notebook.

> *Example:*   Roberto is a student.
> *Is Roberto a student?*

1. He is from Italy.
2. Mr. Peters is his teacher.
3. Roberto and Mr. Peters are in the classroom now.
4. You are busy.
5. The classroom is in a large building.

Exercise E: Simple Present Tense/Negative Form

Please change the affirmative statements to negative statements. Write the negative statements in your notebook.

> *Example:*   Roberto is a teacher.
> *Roberto is not a teacher.*

1. Mr. Peters is near the window.
2. You are nineteen years old.
3. Roberto and Mr. Peters are in a small building.
4. The classroom is large.
5. Mr. Peters is from Italy.

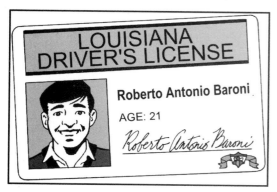

1. _____

2. _____

3. _____

4. _____

5. _____

6. _____

7. _____

8. _____

9. _____

10. _____

11. _____

Model 1 (Narration)

About Me

My name is Roberto Antonio Baroni. My friends call me "Berto." I am twenty-one years old. I am from Italy. I am a student in New Orleans. I study at Lake College. I study English every day. Mr. Peters is my teacher. He is kind and patient. I like him. My classroom is in a large building. It is clean and pleasant. My school is near a large lake. The address is 29 Lake Shore Drive. I like my school.

Caption Writing

Please write a sentence from the model under each picture on page 6, or in your notebook.

Composition 1

Instructions for Student's Composition

1. Write one paragraph about yourself and your school setting on 8 1/2 x 11 inch loose-leaf notebook paper.

2. Follow the model, but change all information that is not correct for you. For example: you are not Mr. Baroni; your first name is probably not Roberto.

3. Take as many structures and words from the model as you can use in your paragraph.

Your composition should look like this:

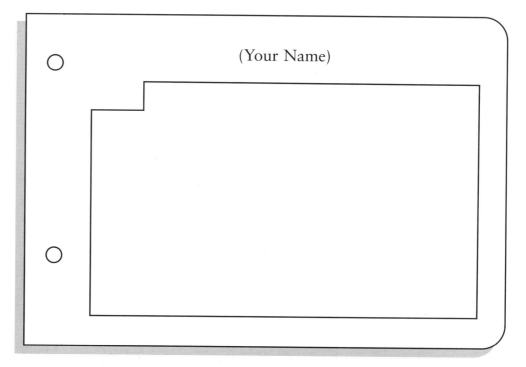

(Your Name)

 # Connecting

Use a search engine (such as Netscape, Yahoo, or Excite). Type in the name of your school and search. Are there any listings? Open a listing. What is it about? Tell a partner about it.

Identifying Family and Home

- Composition Focus: Narration and Description

- Organizational Focus: Division

- Grammatical Focus: Simple Present Tense (all verbs)
  There is/are

1. _____

2. _____

3. _____

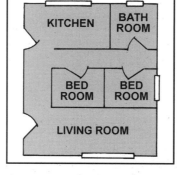

4. _____

5. _____

6. _____

7. _____

8. _____

9. _____

10. _____

Reading 2

Before You Read

Think about this. Talk about it with a partner or group.

Where do you live—in a *house* or in an *apartment?*
What rooms are in your house or apartment? Is there a...?

bedroom	*living room*	*kitchen*	*driveway*
bathroom	*dining room*	*garage*	*yard*

Is your house or apartment...?

large	*comfortable*	*beautiful*	*clean*

Read

The Baroni Family

The Baroni family lives at 3904 Canal Street in New Orleans. There are four members in the family. They are Mr. and Mrs. Baroni and their two children, Roberto and Bruno.

The Baroni family lives in a small apartment. The apartment isn't elegant, but it is comfortable. It has two bedrooms, a living room, a kitchen, and a bathroom. All of the rooms are small. In front of the apartment, there is a small yard. There are beautiful flowers around the apartment. There is a small garage in back of the apartment.

Mr. Baroni is a computer technician. He works in the office of a factory. He likes to watch TV when he has free time. Mrs. Baroni works in a large office downtown. She is a bilingual secretary. She likes to read when she has free time. Roberto and Bruno go to Lake College. They are good students and they study hard.

The Baronis are a nice family. They are busy and they work hard.

After You Read

Caption Writing: Please write a sentence from the reading under each picture on page 10, or in your notebook.

Exercise A: Simple Present Tense/ Comprehension

Please answer the questions in complete sentences.

> *Example:* Where does the Baroni family live?
> *The Baroni family lives at 3904 Canal Street in New Orleans.*

1. How many members are there in the family?

   _____

2. How many rooms does the apartment have?

   _____

3. What is there in front of the apartment?

   _____

4. What is there in back of the apartment?

   _____

5. Where does Mr. Baroni work?

   _____

6. What does Mr. Baroni like to do?

   _____

7. Where does Mrs. Baroni work?

   _____

8. What does Mrs. Baroni like to do?

   _____

9. What are Bruno and Roberto?

   _____

10. How do they study?

   _____

Exercise B: Vocabulary

Part 1

Please choose a word for each blank from the list below.

driveway	*bedroom*	*living room*	*kitchen*	*dining room*
bathroom	*garage*	*yard*	*house*	*apartment*

1. The Baronis live in an _____. They don't live in
   a _____.
2. They watch TV or visit with friends in their _____.
3. Roberto and Bruno sleep in their _____.
4. The family cooks in the _____.
5. Roberto takes a shower in the _____ every
   morning.
6. The family eats in the kitchen. They don't have a
   _____.
7. There are flowers, grass, and trees in the _____.
8. In back of the apartment, there is a small _____
   for the car.
9. The Baronis don't always park their car in the garage. They
   often leave it in the _____.

Part 2

Please find the word with the **opposite** meaning. Write it below.

large	*comfortable*	*patient*	*young*	*back*
front	*beautiful*	*clean*	*kind*	*happy*

1. The flowers are *ugly*. _____
2. In *back* of the apartment,
   there is a yard. _____
3. Mrs. Baroni works in a *small* office. _____
4. Roberto and Bruno are *old*. _____
5. In *front* of their apartment,
   there is a garage. _____
6. Their apartment is usually *dirty*. _____
7. Their home is *uncomfortable*. _____
8. The Baronis are a *sad* family. _____
9. Roberto's teacher is *unkind*. _____
10. His teacher is also *impatient*. _____

Exercise C: Simple Present Tense/Sentence Formation

Please use the words in each group to make a sentence. You may need to add other words and change the verb form.

Example: The Baroni family / live / 3904 Canal Street.
The Baroni family lives at 3904 Canal Street.

1. The apartment / have / two bedrooms.

   _____

2. There / be / four members / the family.

   _____

3. He / like / to watch / TV.

   _____

4. The family / live / a small apartment.

   _____

5. Roberto and Bruno / study / hard.

   _____

6. She / like / to read.

   _____

7. Mrs. Baroni / be / a bilingual secretary.

   _____

8. Mr. Baroni / work / office / factory.

   _____

9. There / be / small yard.

   _____

Exercise D: Order

Please number the following sentences in the correct *order.* Then write the sentences in order on the lines below the exercise.

_____ The school is near their house.

_____ They go to a public school.

_____ The house is on Canal Street.

___1___ The Baronis have two children, Bruno and Roberto.

_____

_____

_____

_____

_____ There is also a tree in the yard.

_____ There are flowers in the yard.

_____ It is tall.

_____ They are beautiful.

_____

_____

_____

_____

_____ She works until 5:00.

_____ She goes home by bus.

_____ In the evening, she goes to bed early.

_____ In the morning, Mrs. Baroni goes to work.

_____

_____

_____

_____

1. _____

2. _____

3. _____

4. _____

5. _____

6. _____

7. _____

8. _____

9. _____

10. _____

11. _____

12. _____

Model 2 (Narration and Description)

My Family

My family lives in New Orleans, Louisiana. My family name is Baroni. My family is from Rome, Italy. My grandparents live in Rome, but my parents, my brother, and I live in New Orleans. It is our new home. We live in a small apartment. It isn't fancy, but it is comfortable. My grandparents have a large house in Rome. My unmarried uncle lives with them. He has his own bedroom. I share a bedroom with my brother.

My father works in the office of a factory. He is a computer technician. My mother is a bilingual secretary. She works in an office, too. She likes books and flowers. My brother, Bruno, is a student. He is also a musician. He plays the violin and the drums in a band. I am a student, too. I don't play the violin but I play soccer. I am a good goalie.

I like my family. I see my parents and my brother every day, but I miss my grandparents very much.

Caption Writing

Please write a sentence from the model under each picture on page 16, or in your notebook.

Composition 2

Instructions for Student's Composition

1. Write three paragraphs about your family on 8 1/2 x 11 inch loose-leaf notebook paper. Remember to indent and leave margins.

2. Put the following information in your composition:

    PARAGRAPH 1.   Introduce your family.
    PARAGRAPH 2.   Tell about their lives. Tell about your life too.
    PARAGRAPH 3.   Tell about your feelings toward your family.

3. Take as many structures and words from the model as you can use in your composition.

Your composition should look like this:

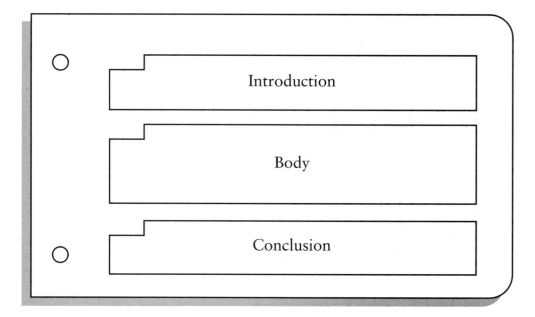

Connecting

Use a search engine (such as Netscape, Yahoo, or Excite). Type in "houses," "apartments," or "real estate." Can you find some places for sale or rent? Choose a house or apartment that you like. Tell a partner about it.

Describing a Typical Activity

🔦 **Composition Focus:** Narration and Description

🔦 **Organizational Focus:** Chronological Order and Division

🔦 **Grammatical Focus:** Simple Present Tense
Frequency Words *(sometimes, always)*

1. _____

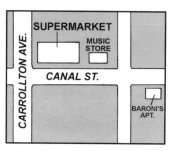

2. _____

3. _____

4. _____

5. _____

6. _____

7. _____

8. _____

9. _____

10. _____

11. _____

12. _____

Reading 3

Before You Read

Think about this. Talk about it with a partner or group.

What *fruit* do you like? Do you like *apples? bananas? oranges?*
Do you like *vegetables*? Do you like *corn? green beans? carrots?*
Do you eat *meat*? Do you eat *beef? chicken? lamb?*
Where do you buy food? Is there a supermarket in your
neighborhood?

Read

Shopping

Mr. and Mrs. Baroni go shopping every Saturday. They like
to go to a large supermarket near their home. It is convenient.
They park their car in the large parking lot. Their sons usually
go with them.

First, they go into the supermarket. Roberto usually pushes
the cart. Mrs. Baroni reads the shopping list. Mr. Baroni and
Bruno look for the groceries. Bruno often forgets an item when
he sees a pretty girl. They almost always buy vegetables, fruit,
meat, eggs, and cheese. The shopping list is usually long. They
do their shopping for the entire week. Many families shop on
Saturdays. The checkout line is always long.

After shopping, Roberto and Bruno usually go to the music
store next door. They look for interesting CDs. Roberto likes
rock music. Bruno likes jazz and classical music. They sometimes
buy a CD. Their parents wait in the car. Their mother is usually
impatient. She wants to go home. The meat and eggs need to
go in the refrigerator.

Everyone helps with the groceries when they arrive home.
The boys carry them to the house. Mr. and Mrs. Baroni put
them away. Then they rest or have lunch.

After You Read

Caption Writing: Please write a sentence from the reading under
each picture on page 20, or in your notebook.

Exercise A: Simple Present Tense/ Comprehension

Please answer the questions in complete sentences.

1. When do the Baronis go shopping?

   _____

2. Where do they park their car?

   _____

3. Where do they go first?

   _____

4. What does Roberto do in the supermarket?

   _____

5. What does Mrs. Baroni do in the supermarket?

   _____

6. What do Mr. Baroni and Bruno do?

   _____

7. When does Bruno forget an item?

   _____

8. What do they buy?

   _____

9. Where do Bruno and Roberto go after shopping?

   _____

10. What do they look for?

   _____

11. Where do their parents wait?

   _____

12. Where does Mrs. Baroni want to go?

   _____

Exercise B: Vocabulary

Part 1

Please choose a word with the *same* meaning. Write it below.

items	*convenient*	*many*	*entire*
near	*vegetables*	*fruit*	*meat*

1. The Baronis do their shopping   _____
   for the *whole* week.

2. They go to a supermarket *close to*   _____
   their apartment.

3. It is *easy* to shop there.   _____

4. They buy many *things* in the supermarket.   _____

5. They buy *apples, bananas,* and *oranges.*   _____

6. They buy *beef* and *chicken.*   _____

7. They also buy *corn, green beans,*   _____
   and *carrots.*

8. *A lot of* families shop on Saturday.   _____

Part 2

Please find the correct words. (Check **Reading 3** for meaning.)

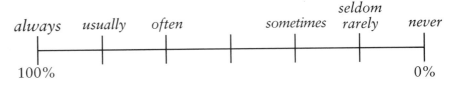

1. The Baronis _____ go shopping on Saturday.

2. They _____ go shopping on Wednesday.

3. Roberto and Bruno _____ go shopping with
   their parents.

4. Roberto _____ pushes the shopping cart.

5. Bruno _____ forgets an item when he sees a
   pretty girl.

6. They almost _____ buy meat, fruit, vegetables,
   eggs, and cheese.

7. Their shopping list is _____ short.

8. The checkout line is _____ short.

9. After shopping, Roberto and Bruno _____ go
   to the music store.

10. They _____ buy a CD.

Exercise C: Simple Present Tense/ Interrogative Form

Please change the statements to questions.

> *Example:* Mrs. Baroni always buys vegetables.
> *Does Mrs. Baroni always buy vegetables?*

1. Mr. and Mrs. Baroni go shopping every Saturday.

   _____

2. Many families shop on Saturday.

   _____

3. Roberto usually pushes the cart.

   _____

4. Bruno often forgets an item.

   _____

5. They usually buy fruit and eggs.

   _____

6. Bruno likes classical music.

   _____

7. Everyone helps with the groceries.

   _____

8. The boys carry the groceries to the apartment.

   _____

Exercise D: Order

Please number the following sentences in the correct *order.* Then write the sentences in order on the lines below the exercise.

_____ Then, Bruno and Roberto go to the music store.

_____ First, the Baronis go to the supermarket.

_____ They look at CDs.

_____ They buy meat and vegetables there.

_____

_____

_____

_____

_____ Everyone helps when they get home.

_____ The parents put them away in the kitchen.

_____ The Baronis drive home from the supermarket.

_____ The boys carry the groceries from the car to the apartment.

_____

_____

_____

_____

1. _____

2. _____

3. _____

4. _____

5. _____

6. _____

7. _____

8. _____

Model 3 (Narration and Description)

My Grandmother's Shopping

My grandmother goes shopping every day. She doesn't work and she has time to shop. She usually buys many different things. She goes from shop to shop with her basket. In her neighborhood in Italy, there are no supermarkets.

At the grocery store, she buys milk, fruit, vegetables, and meat. She doesn't buy very much. She buys these same items every day. They are always fresh. At the drugstore, she often buys toothpaste, soap, or medicine for my grandfather. He is often sick. She goes to the hardware store if she needs nails or screws. She likes to fix things around the house.

She goes to a small cafe after she finishes her shopping. She is usually tired and she stops to rest. Some of her old friends are usually there. They drink coffee and gossip.

Caption Writing

Please write a sentence from the model under each picture on page 26, or in your notebook.

Composition 3

Instructions for Student's Composition

1. Write three paragraphs about your family on 8 1/2 x 11 inch loose-leaf notebook paper. Remember to indent and leave margins. Write about yourself or someone you know.

2. Put the following information in your composition:

   PARAGRAPH 1.   Tell where you or others go shopping.
   PARAGRAPH 2.   Tell what you or others usually buy or look at.
   PARAGRAPH 3.   Tell what happens after shopping.

3. Take as many structures and words from the model as you can use in your composition.

Your composition should look like this:

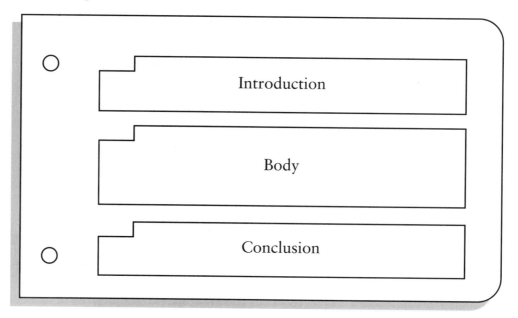

 # Connecting

Use a search engine (such as Netscape, Yahoo, or Excite). Can you find some online grocery stores? What items can people buy? Make a list—tell a partner about the items and their prices.

Describing a Special Place or Event

- Composition Focus: Description and Narration

- Organizational Focus: Spatial and Chronological Order

- Grammatical Focus: Simple Present Tense
  There is/are

1. _____

2. _____

3. _____

4. _____

5. _____

6. _____

7. _____

8. _____

9. _____

10. _____

11. _____

12. _____

Reading 4

Before You Read

Think about this. Talk about it with a partner or group.

What do you do on *special* occasions?
Do you like to listen to music? eat out? stay home?

Read

China Jade

It is Mrs. Baroni's birthday. Mr. and Mrs. Baroni are at their favorite Chinese restaurant, China Jade. They do not go out to eat very often. It is expensive to eat out. They only eat out on special occasions. Mrs. Baroni is forty years old today, so it is a very special occasion.

China Jade is small and elegant. There are about ten tables against the walls. There is a red rose on each table. There is also a beautiful white tablecloth on each table. There are pictures on the walls and plants in the corners. The restaurant is very clean and beautiful.

Yan is the headwaiter. He works very hard and he enjoys his job. He likes the customers and they like him. He knows that it is Mrs. Baroni's birthday and he wants the dinner to be very special. He brings Mr. and Mrs. Baroni a menu and a pot of tea. Then he helps them order. They order soup for their first course. For their main course, they order Peking duck. After the main course, they want a salad. For dessert, they want fruit and coffee. Yan brings them their food. They eat slowly and leisurely. They listen to classical music while they eat. The food is delicious and Yan takes good care of them. They always leave a nice tip when Yan gives them special attention.

The evening is perfect. It is midnight when the Baronis get home. Roberto and Bruno are already asleep. Mrs. Baroni puts her red rose from China Jade in a vase. She is very happy. She thinks that it is not so bad to be forty years old!

After You Read

Caption Writing: Please write a sentence from the reading under each picture on page 30, or in your notebook.

Exercise A: Capitalization

Please rewrite and put *capital letters* where they belong.

---

china jade

it is mrs. baroni's birthday. mr. and mrs. baroni are at their favorite chinese restaurant, china jade. they do not go out to eat very often. it is expensive to eat out. they only eat out on special occasions. mrs. baroni is forty years old today, so it is a very special occasion.

china jade is small and elegant. there are about ten tables against the walls. there is a red rose on each table. there is also a beautiful white tablecloth on each table. there are pictures on the walls and plants in the corners. the restaurant is very clean and beautiful.

yan is the headwaiter. he works very hard and he enjoys his job. he likes the customers and they like him. he knows that it is mrs. baroni's birthday and he wants the dinner to be very special. he brings the baronis a menu and a pot of tea. then he helps them order. they order soup for their first course. for their main course, they order peking duck. after the main course, they want a salad. for dessert, they want fruit and coffee. yan brings them their food. they eat slowly and leisurely. they listen to classical music while they eat. the food is delicious and yan takes good care of them. they always leave a nice tip when yan gives them special attention.

the evening is perfect. it is midnight when the baronis get home. roberto and bruno are already asleep. mrs. baroni puts her red rose from china jade in a vase. she is very happy. she thinks that it is not so bad to be forty years old!

Exercise B: Vocabulary

Part 1

Please use these words in the sentences below.

tip	*elegant*	*special*
birthday	*perfect*	*midnight*
hard	*against*	*menu*

1. It is _____ when the Baronis get home.

2. They only eat out on _____ occasions.

3. It is Mrs. Baroni's _____ today.

4. Yan works very _____ but he likes his job.

5. Yan brings the Baronis a _____.

6. There are about ten tables _____ the walls.

7. They always leave a big _____ when the service is good.

8. It is a _____ evening.

9. China Jade is an _____ restaurant.

Part 2

Please use these words in the sentences below.

at	*of*	*in*
to	*for*	*with*
on		

1. The Baronis are _____ a Chinese restaurant.

2. They order a pot _____ tea.

3. They drink tea _____ their dinner.

4. There is a red rose _____ each table.

5. They order fruit _____ dessert.

6. There are plants _____ the corners.

7. The waiter wants the dinner _____ be very special.

Exercise C: Frequency Words/Word Order

Please rewrite each of the following sentences. Add the frequency word in parentheses to the sentence. Put the *frequency word* next to the verb. Be careful with the *word order.*

Example: The Baronis go out to eat on Saturday. (sometimes)
The Baronis sometimes go out to eat on Saturday.

1. The Baronis eat out on special occasions. (usually)

   _____

2. The Chinese restaurant is very clean. (always)

   _____

3. Yan works hard. (always)

   _____

4. The Baronis order tea. (often)

   _____

5. They order duck. (sometimes)

   _____

6. They eat slowly and leisurely. (always)

   _____

7. For dessert, they have fruit. (sometimes)

   _____

8. After dinner, they have coffee. (usually)

   _____

9. They leave a big tip. (always)

   _____

10. It is midnight when the Baronis get home. (usually)

    _____

Exercise D: Making a Chart

Please fill in words from the reading to complete the cluster chart about Mrs. Baroni's favorite Chinese restaurant.

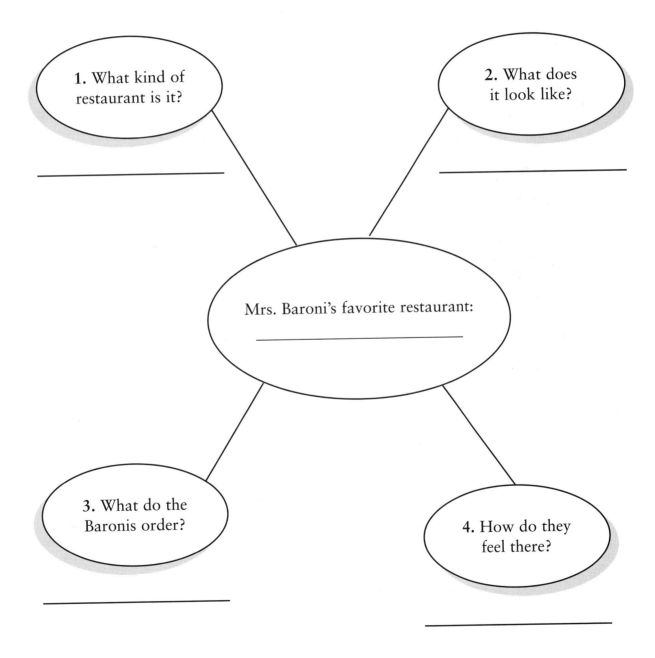

1. What kind of restaurant is it?

_____

2. What does it look like?

_____

Mrs. Baroni's favorite restaurant:

_____

3. What do the Baronis order?

_____

4. How do they feel there?

_____

1. _____

2. _____

3. _____

4. _____

5. _____

6. _____

7. _____

8. _____

Model 4 (Description and Narration)

Katie's

Roberto likes to eat out. He goes to a restaurant for dinner almost every weekend. He doesn't wait for a special occasion. He usually invites his girlfriend, Sylvia, to go with him.

Roberto's favorite restaurant is Katie's. It's a small neighborhood place on Bienville Street. It is not elegant, but it is very pleasant. Katie's granddaughter and her husband run the restaurant. They know most of their customers. They are very friendly. It is a typical New Orleans restaurant. There are only a few tables in the restaurant. There are no tablecloths on the tables. There are posters of New Orleans on the walls. There is a bar in the front. Near the bar, there is a jukebox. The food is delicious. Roberto sometimes orders fried shrimp or oysters. Sylvia likes their fried trout. They eat slowly and leisurely. They always enjoy their meal. The waitresses are friendly and the service is quick. Roberto always leaves a nice tip.

Roberto has a pleasant evening when he goes to his favorite restaurant. He always enjoys an evening with Sylvia at Katie's.

Caption Writing

Please write a sentence from the model under each picture on page 36, or in your notebook.

Composition 4

Instructions for Student's Composition

1. Write three paragraphs about yourself and your favorite restaurant on 8 1/2 x 11 inch loose-leaf notebook paper. Remember to indent and leave margins.

2. Put the following from your cluster chart in your composition:

    PARAGRAPH 1.   What is the name of the restaurant? When do you go there? Who goes with you?

    PARAGRAPH 2.   What kind of restaurant is it? What does it look like? What do you order?

    PARAGRAPH 3.   What kind of evening do you have there? How do you feel?

3. Take as many structures and words from the model as you can use in your composition.

Your composition should look like this:

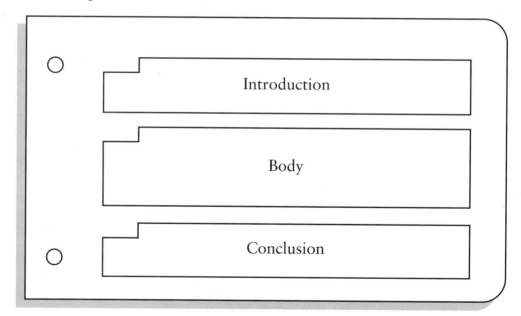

 # Connecting

Use a search engine (such as Netscape, Yahoo, or Excite). Look for restaurants in your town or city. Can you find any restaurant menus? What would you order at the restaurant? Tell a partner about the restaurant.

Describing a Typical Activity

🌳 **Composition Focus:** Description

🌳 **Organizational Focus:** Spatial Order and Division

🌳 **Grammatical Focus:** Simple Present Tense
There is/are
Present Continuous Tense
Quantifiers *(some, many, others)*

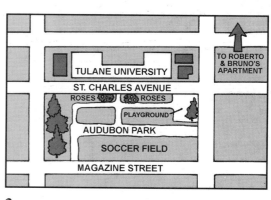

1. _____

2. _____

3. _____

4. _____

5. _____

6. _____

7. _____

8. _____

9. _____

10. _____

11. _____

40 ● **BOOK 1 • Unit 5**

Reading 5

Before You Read

Think about this. Talk about it with a partner or group.

What do you see in the *park*? What do people do in the park? Do they *talk*? *play* sports? *ride* bicycles? *jog*? Do you like to go to the park? Why or why not?

Read

Audubon Park
by Roberto Baroni

On Saturday afternoons, my brother and I like to go to Audubon Park. It is not far from our home. It is near Tulane University. It is between St. Charles Avenue and Magazine Street.

Audubon Park is large and beautiful. There are huge trees in the park. Some are oak and some are magnolia. The trees are tall and give a lot of shade. There are many azalea bushes in the park. In the spring, there are beautiful pink flowers on the bushes. There is also a lot of thick green grass. Near the St. Charles entrance, there are roses.

It is a sunny day and there are many people in the park today. Some of the people are sitting on benches and talking to their friends. There are all kinds of people in the park. Some look rich and some look poor. Some are young and some are old. Some are fat and some are thin. Some look happy and some look sad. Some young people are playing soccer. My brother, Bruno, is playing with them. Others are riding bicycles. A few are jogging. There are some small children on the playground in the park. Some are climbing and some are swinging. Others are running and jumping. The children's mothers and fathers are watching them. One mother is calling to her child because he is running near the street.

Audubon Park is a wonderful place to spend the afternoon.

After You Read

Caption Writing: Please write a sentence from the reading under each picture on page 40, or in your notebook.

Exercise A: Vocabulary

1. Please list the words (from Reading 5) that tell you the activities in the park.

   a. _____*sitting*_____   g. _____

   b. _____   h. _____

   c. _____   i. _____

   d. _____   j. _____

   e. _____   k. _____

   f. _____

2. What are the different categories of plants in the park?

   a. _____   c. _____

   b. _____   d. _____

3. What are the words that describe the plants?

   a. The oak and magnolia trees are _____.

   b. There is also a lot of _____ _____ grass.

   c. There are _____ pink flowers on the bushes.

4. What are the two kinds of flowers in the park?

   a. _____   b. _____

5. What are the two kinds of trees in the park?

   a. _____   b. _____

Exercise B: Present Continuous Tense/ Interrogative Form

Please change the statements to questions. Write the questions in your notebook.

   Example: Some of the people are sitting on benches.
   Are some of the people sitting on benches?

1. Some young people are playing soccer.

2. Bruno is playing with them.

3. Others are riding bicycles.

4. Some children are climbing.

5. One mother is calling to her child.

Exercise C: Recognition

1. In your notebook, please copy each sentence from Reading 5 that contains *there is* or *there are*. (There are eight sentences.)

2. In your notebook, please copy the part of the reading that introduces the subject of Roberto's report.

3. In your notebook, please copy the part that "closes" the reading.

Exercise D: Punctuation

Please rewrite and add the necessary *punctuation.* (You need to add 31 periods.)

Audubon Park
by Roberto Baroni

On Saturday afternoons, my brother and I like to go to Audubon Park It is not far from our home It is near Tulane University It is between St Charles Avenue and Magazine Street

Audubon Park is large and beautiful There are huge trees in the park Some are oak and some are magnolia The trees are tall and give a lot of shade There are many azalea bushes in the park In the spring, there are beautiful pink flowers on the bushes There is also a lot of thick green grass Near the St Charles entrance, there are roses

It is a sunny day and there are many people in the park today Some of the people are sitting on benches and talking to their friends There are all kinds of people in the park Some look rich and some look poor Some are young and some are old Some are fat and some are thin Some look happy and some look sad Some young people are playing soccer Bruno is playing with them Others are riding bicycles A few are jogging There are some small children on the playground in the park Some are climbing and some are swinging Others are running and jumping The children's mothers and fathers are watching them One mother is calling to her child because he is running near the street

Audubon Park is a wonderful place to spend the afternoon

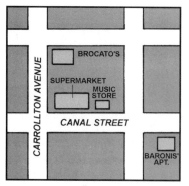

1. _____

2. _____

3. _____

4. _____

5. _____

6. _____

7. _____

8. _____

9. _____

10. _____

11. _____

Model 5 (Description)

Brocato's

Roberto loves ice cream. He especially loves Brocato's ice cream. He says that it is the best ice cream in the world! Roberto often goes to Brocato's after school. It is on Carrollton Avenue near his apartment.

Brocato's is an old-fashioned ice cream shop. Angelo Brocato's grandson runs the shop now. In the windows, there are Italian flags and delicious pastries. Inside, there are small, round marble tables. To the side there is a tall case full of pastries. On top of the case, there are large jars of candy. Next to the pastry case, there are large, round tubs of ice cream in a large refrigerated case.

It is a busy day and there are many people at Brocato's today. Roberto is there with Sylvia. They are eating ice cream and talking about their English test tomorrow. Other people are drinking Italian coffee and reading newspapers. Some look tired. They are probably taking a break from work. Some children are standing at the ice cream case. They are choosing a flavor. Their father is waiting patiently.

Roberto feels comfortable in Brocato's. Mr. Brocato is friendly and the ice cream is the best in the world.

 ## Caption Writing

Please write a sentence from the model under each picture on page 44, or in your notebook.

Composition 5

Instructions for Student's Composition

1. Describe a familiar place where there are activities in progress. Write four paragraphs about the place on 8 1/2 x 11 inch loose-leaf notebook paper. Remember to indent and leave margins.

2. Put the following information in your composition:

   PARAGRAPH 1. Identify the place. Where is it?
   PARAGRAPH 2. Describe the place.
   PARAGRAPH 3. What are the people doing? How do they look?
   PARAGRAPH 4. What is the general atmosphere of the place?

3. Take as many structures and words from the model as you can use in your composition.

4. The different parts of your composition should relate to each other in the following way:

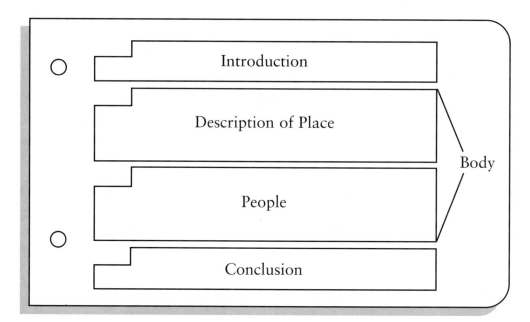

 # Connecting

Use a search engine (such as Netscape, Yahoo, or Excite). Can you find information about an interesting park or hiking areas near your town or city? Where is it? What do people do there? Tell a partner about the place.

Describing Locations

🔎 **Composition Focus: Description**

🔎 **Organizational Focus: Spatial Order**

🔎 **Grammatical Focus: Simple Present Tense**
There is/are
Prepositions

1. _____

2. _____

3. _____

4. _____

5. _____

6. _____

7. _____

8. _____

9. _____

Reading 6

Before You Read

Think about this. Talk about it with a partner or group.

Where do you buy food—in a *supermarket* or in a small *grocery store?* Close your eyes and think of the store. What is *on the right? on the left? near the back* of the store? What do you *see?* What do you *smell?*

Read

The Whole Food Company

Sylvia Gomez, Roberto's girlfriend, doesn't like to shop at a supermarket. She prefers to shop at a small grocery store, The Whole Food Company. It is a small, friendly store in her neighborhood.

Sylvia feels good the moment she enters the store. Everywhere she sees beautiful green plants. To her right, she sees a long case of fresh fruit and vegetables. The colors are beautiful. There are yellow lemons next to red apples and orange carrots next to green peppers. Near the back, there is a small case of yogurt, eggs, cheese, and milk. Next to the dairy case, there is a tall case of fresh meat. The butcher always says hello, and Sylvia sometimes buys fresh fish or beef.

On the opposite side, there are rows of shelves. The shelves are full of bottles of oil, boxes of crackers, and bags of fresh coffee beans. The coffee beans smell wonderful. In the far corner, near the front, there is a small bakery counter. The fresh bread smells wonderful, too. Next to the bakery counter, there are big vases of fresh flowers. Sylvia usually buys some for her apartment. The checkout counter is next to the fresh flowers. The cashier always says hello.

Sylvia loves this store. The colors are beautiful. The smells are wonderful. The people are friendly.

After You Read

Caption Writing: Please write a sentence from the reading under each picture on page 48, or in your notebook.

Exercise A: Prepositions

Please add the correct *prepositions*.

to	*for*	*of*	*at*
on	*in*	*next to*	

Sylvia Gomez, Roberto's girlfriend, doesn't like _____
shop _____ a supermarket. She prefers _____
shop _____ a small grocery store, The Whole Food
Company. It is a small, friendly store _____ her
neighborhood.

Sylvia feels good the moment she enters the store. Everywhere
she sees beautiful green plants. _____ her right, she sees a
long case _____ fresh fruit and vegetables. The colors are
beautiful. There are yellow lemons _____ red apples and
orange carrots _____ green peppers. Near the back, there
is a small case _____ yogurt, eggs, cheese, and milk.

_____ the dairy case, there is a tall case _____
fresh meat. The butcher always says hello, and Sylvia sometimes
buys fresh fish or beef.

_____ the opposite side, there are rows
_____ shelves. The shelves are full of bottles
_____ oil, boxes _____ crackers, and bags
_____ fresh coffee beans. The coffee beans smell
wonderful. _____ the far corner, near the front, there is a
small bakery counter. The fresh bread smells wonderful, too.

_____ the bakery counter, there are big vases
_____ fresh flowers. Sylvia usually buys some
_____ her apartment. The checkout counter is
_____ the fresh flowers. The cashier always says hello.

Sylvia loves this store. The colors are beautiful. The smells are
wonderful. The people are friendly.

Exercise B: Order

Please number the following sentences in the correct *order*. Then write the sentences in order in your notebook.

A.

> _____ The apples and oranges are especially fresh and beautiful.
>
> _____ The fruit is near the entrance.
>
> _____ The tomatoes and green peppers are on sale today.
>
> _____ The vegetables are next to the fruit.

B.

> _____ The butcher is friendly and helpful.
>
> _____ The case is full of fresh yogurt, milk, eggs, and cheese.
>
> _____ Next to the dairy case, you can find fresh meat.
>
> _____ Near the back, there is a small dairy case.

C.

> _____ Next to the coffee, there is a small bakery counter.
>
> _____ The fresh bread smells wonderful.
>
> _____ Along the side wall, there are rows of shelves.
>
> _____ The shelves are full of oil, crackers, and coffee.

Exercise C: Recognition

1. In your notebook, please copy the *introduction* to Reading 6. (It's the first paragraph.)

2. The second and third paragraphs are the *body* of the reading. What area of space (part of the store) is described in those two paragraphs?

   a. The second paragraph describes_____.

   b. The third paragraph describes _____.

3. In your notebook, please copy the *conclusion* to the reading. (It's the fourth paragraph.)

4. In your notebook, please copy each sentence that contains *there is* or *there are.* (There are six sentences.)

1. _____

2. _____

3. _____

4. _____

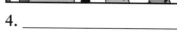

5. _____

6. _____

7. _____

8. _____

9. _____

10. _____

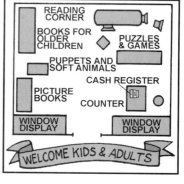

11. _____

Model 6 (Description)

Kid Tales

In Sylvia's neighborhood, there is a small children's bookstore. Sylvia likes to go there. She likes the name of the store—Kid Tales. Sylvia often goes there to buy gifts for her niece and nephew. They live in Mexico City.

The store is bright and cheerful. To the left of the front door, there are large books for young children. The colors are bright and the pictures are beautiful. Sylvia always looks at these first. Her favorite book is *The Sleepy Caterpillar*. Next to the picture books, there are shelves of puppets and soft animals. Sylvia especially likes the teddy bears. Near the toys, there are books for older children. There are shelves and shelves of these books. Sylvia likes to read the titles. Her favorite is *Sixth Grade Gets to You*. In the back, there is a reading corner with a small table and chairs.

On the other side of the store, there are puzzles and games. One puzzle is a map of the United States. Each state is a piece of the puzzle. Sylvia wants to buy one for her niece's birthday. Near the door, there is a counter with a cash register on it. The owner of the store usually sits behind the counter. She is friendly and helpful.

Sylvia likes the store. A children's bookstore is for adults, too!

Caption Writing

Please write a sentence from the model under each picture on page 52, or in your notebook.

Composition 6

Instructions for Student's Composition

1. Choose a place that is familiar to you. Write a physical description of this place. Your composition should contain four paragraphs. Use 8 1/2 x 11 inch loose-leaf notebook paper. Remember to indent and leave margins.

2. Put the following information in your composition:

   PARAGRAPH 1.   Identify the place. Do you work there?
   PARAGRAPH 2.   Divide the area into two parts and describe one half.
   PARAGRAPH 3.   Describe the other half.
   PARAGRAPH 4.   Give a general impression of the place.

3. The different parts of your composition should relate to each other in the following way:

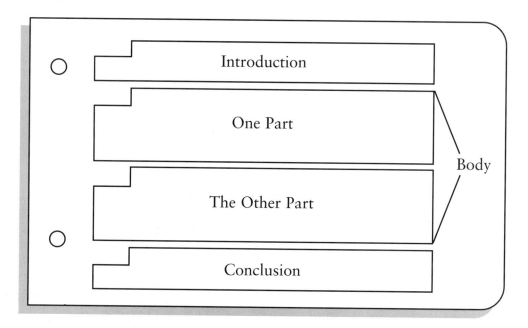

 # Connecting

Use a search engine (such as Netscape, Yahoo, or Excite). Can you find the names of some online bookstores? Are there any interesting books there? Tell a partner about a book that sounds interesting to you.

Describing Activities

🔘 **Composition Focus:** Friendly Letter in Conversational Tone
   Description and Narration

🔘 **Organizational Focus:** Shift of Conversational Scope

🔘 **Grammatical Focus:** Simple Present Tense
   Present Continuous Tense
   Connecting Words

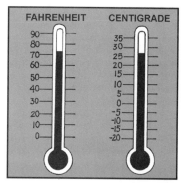

1. _____

2. _____

"NOT TOO HOT, NOT TOO COLD..."

3. _____

4. _____

5. _____

6. _____

7. _____

8. _____

9. _____

10. _____

11. _____

12. _____

Reading 7

Before You Read

Think about this. Talk about it with a partner or group.

Is it *sunny* or *cloudy* today? Is it *hot* or *cold?* What's the *temperature*? Do you like the weather at this time of year? Do you like to write letters? Who do you write to? What do you write about?

Read

May 7, 2002

Dear Grandmother and Grandfather,

It is a nice sunny day in New Orleans and I am sitting in Audubon Park. It is early afternoon and I am thinking of you. The temperature is in the 70s. This is the best time of year in New Orleans because it is not too hot and not too cold. The azaleas are blooming and the air smells fresh and sweet. There are a lot of people in the park. Some of them are strolling while others are sitting on park benches and reading. Several people are riding their bicycles. Bruno is playing soccer with some friends.

We are fine. I have a part-time job in a sporting goods store, but I only work three days a week after school. Bruno also has a part-time job. He works in a music store. The store sells musical instruments. It is a perfect job for him. You know that he is crazy about music! Mom and Dad are fine. They are always busy, too.

I hope that you are fine. Grandfather, how is your health? Is Grandmother taking good care of you? How is the old neighborhood? Do my old friends still remember me? Please say hello to them for me. Also, say hello to Uncle Umberto. Can you read my letters in English? I hope so. Please write soon. My parents and Bruno say hello.

Your grandson,
Roberto

After You Read

Caption Writing: Please write a sentence from the reading under each picture on page 56, or in your notebook.

Sample Envelope

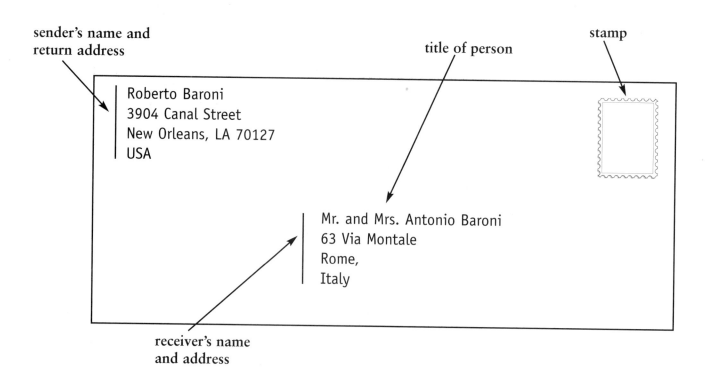

sender's name and return address

title of person

stamp

Roberto Baroni
3904 Canal Street
New Orleans, LA 70127
USA

Mr. and Mrs. Antonio Baroni
63 Via Montale
Rome,
Italy

receiver's name and address

Exercise A: Writing an Envelope

Please complete the envelope. Use your name and address for the sender's name and return address. Use the name and address of a relative or friend for the receiver.

Exercise B: Present Tenses/Comprehension

Please answer the questions in complete sentences.

1. Who is Roberto writing to?

   _____

2. What is the date of the letter?

   _____

3. What season of the year is it?

   _____

4. What is the weather like?

   _____

5. What is Roberto's brother doing?

   _____

6. How are Roberto and his family?

   _____

7. Where do Bruno and Roberto work?

   _____

8. Why is Bruno's job perfect for him?

   _____

9. What does Roberto ask his grandfather about?

   _____

10. How is Roberto related to Mr. and Mrs. Antonio Baroni? (Is he their *cousin*, for example?)

    _____

Exercise C: Sentence Combining

Please combine these sentences. Use the word in parentheses at the end of the first sentence in each group below.

Example: Roberto lives in New Orleans. (but)
His grandparents live in Rome.
Roberto lives in New Orleans, but his grandparents live in Rome.

1. It is a nice day in New Orleans. (and)
Roberto is thinking of his grandparents.

_____

2. The azaleas are blooming. (and)
The air smells sweet and fresh.

_____

3. Some of the people in the park are strolling. (while)
Others are sitting and reading.

_____

4. Roberto is writing a letter. (while)
Bruno is playing soccer.

_____

5. Bruno's job is perfect for him. (because)
He is crazy about music.

_____

6. Roberto's job is perfect for him. (because)
He likes sports.

_____

7. Roberto is asking about his grandfather's health. (because)
His grandfather is often sick.

_____

8. Roberto and Bruno have part-time jobs. (but)
Their parents have full-time jobs.

_____

Exercise D: Order

Please number the following sentences in the correct *order.* Then write the sentences in order in your notebook.

A.

_____	Others are sitting and reading.
_____	There are a lot of people in the park.
_____	In conclusion, all of them are enjoying the nice weather.
_____	Some of them are strolling.

B.

_____	Roberto has a job in a sporting goods store.
_____	However, he meets many interesting people.
_____	The pay is not very good.
_____	They ask him many questions about sports equipment.

C.

_____	The old man is not very well.
_____	He hopes that they still remember him.
_____	First, Roberto asks about his grandfather's health.
_____	Then, he asks about his friends.

D.

_____	He especially likes the violin and the drums.
_____	The store sells musical instruments.
_____	Bruno likes musical instruments.
_____	Roberto's brother works part time in a store.

1. _____

2. _____

3. _____

4. _____

5. _____

6. _____

7. _____

8. _____

9. _____

10. _____

11. _____

12. _____

Model 7 (Friendly Letter)

Sylvia's Letter to a Friend

Tuesday, April 20, 2002

Dear Elsy,

It is 3:00 in the afternoon and I am sitting in the library. It isn't a very nice day. It is raining and I am feeling homesick. I miss my friends and family. There are many students in the library today. Most of them are studying. A few students are sleeping or talking to their friends, but most of them are busy. Roberto, my boyfriend, is here with me. He is studying, too. He is very nice. I want you to meet him when you come to New Orleans.

I am fine. I am learning a lot of English in my classes. Now I can write a letter in English to you! I like my teacher and classmates. Roberto is my favorite classmate! I attend classes five mornings a week and I work three afternoons a week. Today is one of my days off. My cousin, Maria, is fine. She sends greetings to you.

I hope that you are well and happy. When will you come to visit? Please write soon.

Your friend,

Sylvia

NOTE: There are different ways to conclude or close a letter:
- *Love* (when you write to a special friend or relative)
- *Sincerely* (when you write a business letter or write to a friend)
- *Your friend* (when you write to a friend)
- *Your cousin, aunt, uncle, etc.* (when you write to a relative).

 ## Caption Writing

Please write a sentence from the model under each picture on page 62, or in your notebook.

Composition 7

Instructions for Student's Composition

1. Write a three-paragraph letter to someone that you know well: a friend, cousin, brother, etc. Address an envelope to put the letter in. Write the letter on your own personal stationery or a piece of 8 1/2 x 11 inch loose-leaf notebook paper. Don't put your name, course, and the title at the top of the page as you normally do.

2. Write the date in the top right corner of your paper. To the left, 1 1/2 inches down, write *Dear* _____.

    PARAGRAPH 1.   Describe where you are. What are you doing? What are the people around you doing?

    PARAGRAPH 2.   Talk about your daily life.

    PARAGRAPH 3.   Ask about the daily life of the person that you are writing to.

    Before you write your name, use one of these conclusions: *Love, Sincerely, Your friend/cousin/brother,* etc.

3. Your letter should look like this:

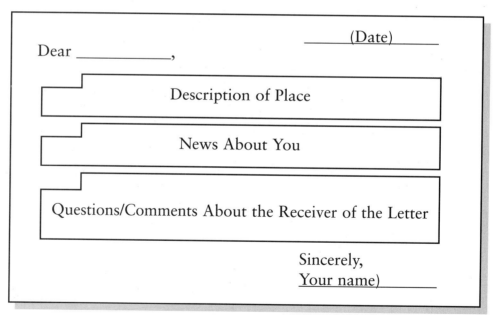

Connecting

Use a search engine (such as Netscape, Yahoo, or Excite). Choose a city. Tell a partner about the weather and temperature there.

Describing Future Activities

🔴 Composition Focus: Narration

🔴 Organizational Focus: Spatial and Chronological Order

🔴 Grammatical Focus: Future
    be going to
    Simple Present Tense
    Quantifiers

1. _____

2. _____

3. _____

4. _____

5. _____

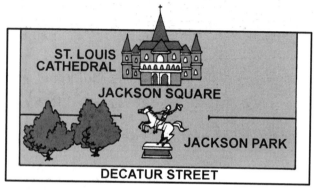

6. _____

7. _____

8. _____

9. _____

10. _____

Reading 8

Before You Read

Think about this. Talk about it with a partner or group.

What are you going to do this weekend?
Do you like *picnics?* What do people bring to and do at picnics?

Read

From: "Sylvia" <smgomez@rivernet.com>
To: "Roberto" <rbaroni5352@worldlink.com>
Subject: Class picnic
Date: May 23, 2002

Hi Roberto,

    We are going to have a class picnic on Saturday in Jackson Park. You are often absent from class so I want to remind you. Please don't forget! We are going to give Mr. Peters a gift. Maria and I are going to choose a book for him. Most of the students are going to be there, but several are going to come later in the afternoon.

    We are going to meet in front of St. Louis Cathedral at 11:00 on Saturday morning. There are usually lots of people in the square. In front of the cathedral, there are many things to see. Some musicians usually play music in the square and people dance. A few magicians do tricks there, too.

    Then, about noon, we are going to walk through the square. There are usually some artists to the side of the square. They hang their paintings on the fence there. I am going to bring my camera and take pictures of them.

    Then we are going to go into the park and find a place to eat. I am going to make some fruit salad. Another student is going to bake a cake. Others are going to bring sandwiches, juice, and chips. Some students are going to bring their favorite CDs.

    It is going to be fun. I think Mr. Peters is going to enjoy it. Please let me know if you are going to come!

Your friend,
Sylvia

After You Read

Caption Writing: Please write a sentence from the reading under each picture on page 66, or in your notebook.

Exercise A: Future *(be going to)*/Comprehension

Please answer the questions in complete sentences.

1. When is the class going to have a picnic?

   _____

2. Where is the picnic going to be?

   _____

3. What are the students going to give Mr. Peters?

   _____

4. When is the class going to meet?

   _____

5. Where do musicians usually play music?

   _____

6. Where are there usually some artists?

   _____

7. Who is going to bring a camera?

   _____

8. What is Sylvia going to make for the picnic?

   _____

9. What are they going to eat at the picnic?

   _____

10. Who is going to bring CDs?

   _____

Exercise B: Recognition

Please answer the following questions about Reading 8.

1. How many paragraphs are there in Sylvia's e-mail? _____

2. Which paragraph introduces the topic? _____

3. Which paragraph concludes the topic? _____

4. How many paragraphs are there in the body? _____

5. What are the points of organization for the body?

   a. _____

   b. _____

   c. _____

6. What verb form is best for *tomorrow, on Saturday,* and *next week,* but not *now* or *every day,* for example?

   _____

7. What tense is best for *every day* or *usually?*

   _____

8. List in the proper category the different activities that you find in Reading 8.

future (*be going to…*)		simple present (*every day, usually*)
a. *are going to*	h. _____	a. *play (music)*
have (a picnic)	i. _____	b. _____
b. _____	j. _____	c. _____
c. _____	k. _____	d. _____
d. _____	l. _____	
e. _____	m. _____	
f. _____	n. _____	
g. _____	o. _____	

Exercise C: Quantifiers

Please rewrite the following sentences. Add the words for quantity to the subject of each sentence.

    Example: People are watching the magician. (many)
                         Many people are watching the magician.

1. Musicians are going to play jazz. (two)

   _____

2. People are going to watch the musicians. (some)

   _____

3. People are going to dance to the music. (several)

   _____

4. People are going to have a picnic. (some)

   _____

5. People are tourists. (many)

   _____

6. Students are going to take pictures. (a few)

   _____

7. Student is going to bake a cake. (one)

   _____

8. Student is going to bring sandwiches. (another)

   _____

9. People are going to watch the artists. (some)

   _____

10. There are activities in Jackson Square. (many)

    _____

Exercise D: Future *(be going to)*/Sentence Formation

Please use the words in each group to make a sentence about the future. Use *be going to.* You may need to add other words and change the verb form.

> *Example:*   The students / have / a picnic.
> *The students are going to have a picnic.*

1. It / be / in Jackson Park.

   _____

2. Maria and Sylvia / buy / a gift / for Mr. Peters.

   _____

3. Most students / arrive / at 11:00.

   _____

4. We / walk / around Jackson Square.

   _____

5. Sylvia / take pictures / of the class.

   _____

6. I / make / a fruit salad.

   _____

7. They / listen to / CDs.

   _____

8. It / be / fun.

   _____

1. _____

2. _____

3. _____

4. _____

5. _____

6. _____

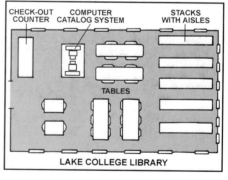

CHECK-OUT COUNTER   COMPUTER CATALOG SYSTEM   STACKS WITH AISLES

TABLES

LAKE COLLEGE LIBRARY

7. _____

8. _____

Model 8 (Narration)

The Library

Notice: To All Students and Staff

The Lake College Library is closed this weekend. The librarians are going to make some changes. The library is going to open again on Monday. The library staff hopes you are going to like the new changes in the library.

Near the entrance to the library, there is going to be a new counter. Several librarians are going to work behind the counter. They are going to answer questions about information and books. One librarian is going to help students with the computer catalog system.

Near the center of the library, there are going to be rows of new tables. Students are going to study and read at these tables. During final exams, many students are going to use this space for study groups.

In the back of the library, there are going to be many more shelves of books. Students are going to find special books for their classes there. The librarians are going to put new signs and posters on the shelves. It is going to be easy to find books on the shelves.

The library is an important place for students and teachers. The librarians think the changes are going to make the library a better place. Your librarians hope you are going to like the changes.

Caption Writing

Please write a sentence from the model under each picture on page 72, or in your notebook.

Composition 8

Instructions for Student's Composition

1. Choose a busy place that is familiar to you. Perhaps you can write about the school cafeteria or the office or factory where you work. Describe the activities that you are *going to see*. Write five paragraphs on 8 1/2 x 11 inch loose-leaf notebook paper.

2. Put the following information in your composition:

    PARAGRAPH 1.   Describe the place and the situation.
    PARAGRAPH 2.   Describe the front area and what is going to happen there.
    PARAGRAPH 3.   Describe the center area and what is going to happen there.
    PARAGRAPH 4.   Describe the back area and what is going to happen there.
    PARAGRAPH 5.   Give a general statement about the place.

3. The different parts of your composition should relate to each other in the following way:

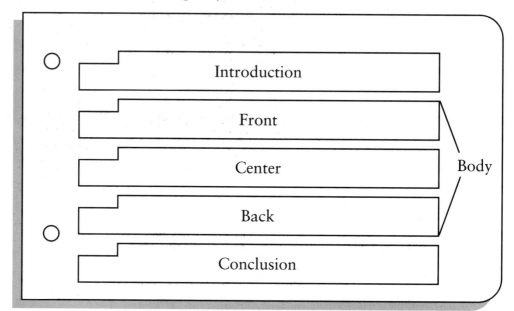

Connecting

Use a search engine (such as Netscape, Yahoo, or Excite). Can you find information about an event (a concert, a festival, a parade) that is going to happen in your city or town? Tell a partner about it.

Describing Future Plans

🔵 **Composition Focus: Narration**

🔵 **Organizational Focus: Chronological Order**

🔵 **Grammatical Focus: Future**
will
Information Questions

1. _____

2. _____

3. _____

4. _____

5. _____

6. _____

7. _____

8. _____

9. _____

10. _____

Reading 9

Before You Read

Think about this. Talk about it with a partner or group.

What kind of work do you do now?
What will you do in ten years? Will you be in school? Will you have a job? Where will you be? Look in your crystal ball!

Read

Roberto's and Bruno's Plans

Roberto and Bruno are still in school. They are thinking about their future. In ten years, they will work full time. They will not have the same jobs. Roberto will be a soccer coach and Bruno will be a jazz musician.

First, Roberto will finish college. He will take classes in science, health, and education. He will not take art or history. Roberto will probably play soccer on the college team. He will be busy but he will enjoy the sports and classes. After college, Roberto will teach in a high school. He will teach science and coach the school's soccer teams. Roberto will love coaching soccer. His teams will work hard and practice every day, of course. They will have fun and maybe they will win a lot of games.

Bruno will start a jazz band. He will not play the keyboard. He will play the drums. The band will practice every day and write their own songs. Bruno's band will probably play in clubs in New Orleans. Maybe the band will record some songs or make a music video. Bruno hopes the band will become rich and famous. Then Bruno and the band will travel and have concerts around the world. Bruno will not forget his family. He will visit them often.

Roberto and Bruno will work hard for their goals. Mr. and Mrs. Baroni like Roberto's plans, but they are not sure about Bruno's plans to be a musician.

After You Read

Caption Writing: Please write a sentence from the reading under each picture on page 76, or in your notebook.

Exercise A: Future *(will)*/Comprehension

Please answer the questions in complete sentences.

1. Do Roberto and Bruno work full time now?

   _____

2. What will Roberto be in ten years?

   _____

3. Who will be a jazz musician?

   _____

4. What classes will Roberto take in college?

   _____

5. When will his soccer teams practice?

   _____

6. Where will Bruno's band play?

   _____

   _____

   _____

   _____

7. What will the band record or make?

   _____

8. Where will the band travel?

   _____

9. Why will the band travel?

   _____

10. Do Mr. and Mrs. Baroni like Roberto's and Bruno's plans?

    _____

Exercise B: Comprehension

Please circle the letter to show the correct information.

1. Roberto and Bruno will work
   a. in different jobs.
   b. with their family.
   c. full time now.

2. Roberto will study and
   a. play in a band.
   b. teach science.
   c. play soccer.

3. Roberto will
   a. become a jazz musician.
   b. be a soccer coach.
   c. work at Security Sporting Goods.

4. Roberto will teach science
   a. at the same time.
   b. before college.
   c. now.

5. Maybe the team will win
   a. every day.
   b. many games.
   c. no games.

6. Bruno's band will write
   a. every day.
   b. songs.
   c. clubs.

7. First, the band will play
   a. in New Orleans.
   b. in concerts around the world.
   c. in music videos.

8. Maybe Bruno's band will
   a. practice every day.
   b. become rich and famous.
   c. like music.

Exercise C: Information Questions

Please write information questions for the sentences.

Example: Roberto and Bruno live in New Orleans.
Where do Roberto and Bruno live?

1. Roberto works after school three days a week.

    How often _____?

2. Bruno works in a music store.

    Where _____?

3. In ten years, Roberto will be a soccer coach.

    When _____?

4. Roberto will coach the school's soccer teams.

    What _____?

5. Bruno will start a jazz band.

    Who _____?

6. The band will play in clubs in New Orleans.

    Where _____?

7. The band will record some songs.

    What _____?

8. The band will have concerts around the world.

    Where _____?

Exercise D: Order

Please number the sentences in the correct *order.* Then write the sentences in order in your notebook.

A.

_____	They study English every day.
_____	They also work three days a week after school.
_____	Now Roberto and Bruno are students at Lake College in New Orleans.
_____	In ten years, Roberto will be a coach and Bruno will be a musician.

B.

_____	Maybe the teams will win a lot of games.
_____	Roberto will finish college and become a teacher.
_____	The soccer teams will work hard and practice every day.
_____	He will also coach high school soccer.

C.

_____	Bruno's parents will be proud of their son's success.
_____	The band will be famous and play concerts around the world.
_____	Bruno's band will probably play in clubs in New Orleans.
_____	Bruno will start a jazz band with some friends.

1. _____

2. _____

3. _____

4. _____

5. _____

6. _____

7. _____

8. _____

Model 9 (Narration)

Sylvia's Plans

Sylvia Gomez lives with her cousin, Maria, in a small apartment. They are both from Mexico City. Sylvia is a student at Lake College and works part time in a department store three afternoons a week. Sylvia likes art. She draws and paints beautiful pictures. She wants to be an artist and writer in the future.

Next year, Sylvia will take art and writing classes in college. She enjoys these kinds of classes. She already has many drawings and pictures and she will draw and paint many more. She will write stories about some of her pictures. Later she will show them to her teacher, Mr. Peters. Maybe he will send her work to the campus magazine. Maybe it will print Sylvia's work.

Sylvia will also send her stories to her cousins in Mexico because they enjoy her stories. Sylvia will feel happy because she likes art and stories.

Caption Writing

Please write a sentence from the model under each picture on page 82, or in your notebook.

Composition 9

Instructions for Student's Composition

1. Write several paragraphs about your future plans. Use 8 1/2 x 11 inch loose-leaf notebook paper. Remember to indent and leave margins.

2. Put the following information in your composition:

   PARAGRAPH 1. What do you do now? Think about your future. What job do you want to have?

   PARAGRAPH 2. Tell about how you will prepare for the job. What will you study or do?

   PARAGRAPH 3. Tell how you (or your family) will feel when you have the job. Tell how you will feel. Will you be rich? happy? famous?

   PARAGRAPH 4. Tell how your family will feel about your future.

3. The different parts of your composition should relate to each other in the following way:

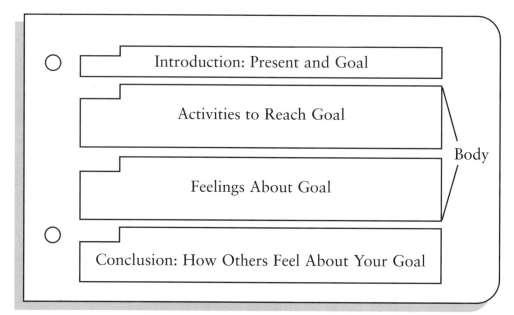

Introduction: Present and Goal

Activities to Reach Goal

Feelings About Goal

Body

Conclusion: How Others Feel About Your Goal

Connecting

Use a search engine (such as Netscape, Yahoo, or Excite). Choose a job or profession that you like. What information can you find about the job? What activities are part of the job? What do you need to know for the job? Tell a partner about the job or profession.

Describing Past Events

🍭 Composition Focus: Narration

🍭 Organizational Focus: Chronological Order

🍭 Grammatical Focus: Simple Past Tense

1. _____

2. _____

3. _____

4. _____

5. _____

6. _____

7. _____

8. _____

9. _____

10. _____

11. _____

12. _____

Reading 10

Before You Read

Think about this. Talk about it with a partner or group.

Do you like to travel? Did you ever travel by *train*? by *plane*? by *car*?
Do you like *sightseeing*? Do you like to visit *museums*? *parks*? *stores*?
Tell about a past trip. Where did you go?

Read

New York! New York!

Mr. and Mrs. Baroni took a trip to New York last month. They went there to visit some friends from their old neighborhood in Rome. Bruno and Roberto stayed in New Orleans. They had to go to school. Mr. and Mrs. Baroni went to New York by plane.

The flight there was very pleasant. They arrived at noon and their friends, the Compagnos, met them at the airport. Their friends were happy to see them. They hugged and kissed and hugged and kissed! While the Baronis got their luggage, Mr. Compagno got the car. Then they all went to the Compagnos' house. They talked and joked all afternoon and had a lovely Italian dinner together that evening. The next day, they got up early and went sightseeing with their friends. They went to Central Park and to the Guggenheim Museum. They also went to the top of the Empire State Building. That evening, they ate dinner at the Compagnos' favorite Italian restaurant. The following day, they visited the United Nations Building and the Statue of Liberty.

The Baronis returned to New Orleans after five wonderful days in New York. They were sad to leave their friends. They invited the Compagnos to come to New Orleans for a visit. They said good-bye many times.

The Baronis were happy to see Bruno and Roberto when they got home. They had a wonderful time in New York, but it was good to be home. The house was clean and the refrigerator was full. Mrs. Baroni was surprised!

After You Read

Caption Writing: Please write a sentence from the reading under each picture on page 86, or in your notebook.

Exercise A: Recognition

Please write the simple verb form for each verb. You may want to check the past tense forms for irregular verbs in the Appendix on page 93.

Example: took   <u>*take*</u>

1. went   _____
2. stayed   _____
3. had to   _____
4. was   _____
5. arrived   _____
6. met   _____
7. were   _____
8. hugged   _____
9. kissed   _____
10. got   _____

11. talked   _____
12. joked   _____
13. drove   _____
14. got up   _____
15. ate   _____
16. visited   _____
17. returned   _____
18. invited   _____
19. said   _____

Exercise B: Simple Past Tense/Comprehension

Please answer the questions with complete sentences.

1. Why did Mr. and Mrs. Baroni go to New York?

   _____

2. Why didn't Bruno and Roberto go?

   _____

3. How did the Baronis get to New York?

   _____

4. How did the Compagnos welcome the Baronis?

   _____

5. How did they get from the airport to the city?

   _____

6. How did the Baronis spend their time in New York? What did they do and see?

   _____

   _____

   _____

   _____

7. How long did the Baronis stay in New York?

_____

8. How did they feel when they left?

_____

9. How did they feel about getting home?

_____

10. How did they find the house?

_____

Exercise C: Connectors

Please use the following *connecting words* in the sentences below.

and	*because*	*but*	*when*
after	*before*	*if*	*while*

1. The Baronis went to New York _____ they wanted to visit their old friends.

2. Bruno and Roberto stayed in New Orleans _____ their parents went to New York.

3. Bruno and Roberto were in New Orleans _____ their parents were in New York.

4. Bruno and Roberto stayed home _____ they had to go to school.

5. The Baronis went to their friends' house _____ they got their luggage.

6. They got up early _____ went sightseeing.

7. They visited the United Nations _____ saw the Statue of Liberty.

8. They also went to the Guggenheim Museum _____ they left New York.

9. The Baronis were sad to leave their friends, _____ they were happy to go home.

10. Roberto and Bruno will go with their parents next time _____ they are not in school.

1. _____

2. _____

3. _____

4. _____

5. _____

6. _____

7. _____

8. _____

9. _____

10. _____

11. _____

Model 10 (Narration)

A Trip to San Francisco

Roberto and Bruno took a trip to San Francisco last July. They went there to visit Dominick. He is a friend from their old neighborhood in Rome. He is also a distant cousin. They went there by train because they wanted to see more of the United States. The trip took two days and nights.

They arrived in San Francisco at midnight. Dominick met them at the train station. They were so happy to see him. He looked exactly the same. They gave him a big hug. The next day, they went sightseeing. They rode the cable cars, saw the Golden Gate Bridge, and had lunch at Fisherman's Wharf. At Fisherman's Wharf, they saw the fishing boats come in. The next day, they visited the University of California at Berkeley. Dominick is a student there. Bruno and Roberto liked the campus. They thought that it was very big and very beautiful.

They saw all of San Francisco before they left. Dominick took them everywhere! They returned to New Orleans by plane because they didn't have time to return by train. Dominick was sad to see them go and they were sad to leave.

All in all, Roberto and Bruno had a wonderful trip. They traveled across Texas, New Mexico, and Arizona. They saw the beautiful coast of California. They toured all of San Francisco. They had a great visit with Dominick. Perhaps they will go again next summer!

Caption Writing

Please write a sentence from the model under each picture on page 90, or in your notebook.

Composition 10

Instructions for Student's Composition

1. Write five paragraphs about a past trip. Use 8 1/2 x 11 inch loose-leaf notebook paper. Remember to indent and leave margins.

2. Put the following information in your composition:

    PARAGRAPH 1.   Where did you go on your trip? When did you go? Why did you go there? How did you go? How long did the trip take?

    PARAGRAPH 2.   Tell about your arrival.

    PARAGRAPH 3.   What did you do after you arrived?

    PARAGRAPH 4.   Tell about your return home.

    PARAGRAPH 5.   Tell your feelings about the trip.

3. The different parts of your composition should relate to each other as in:

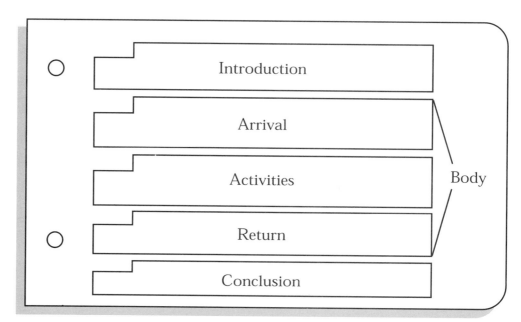

 # Connecting

Use a search engine (such as Netscape, Yahoo, or Excite). Choose a city in the United States that you want to visit. What places can you visit there? What can you do? Check plane and train schedules and fares. Tell a partner about the city and places to visit.

Appendix

Irregular verbs from Unit 10

Present	Past
be	was/were
do	did
drive	drove
eat	ate
feel	felt
find	found
get	got
give	gave
go	went
have	had
leave	left
meet	met
ride	rode
say	said
see	saw
spend	spent
take	took
think	thought

Skills Index

LANGUAGE (Grammar, Usage, and Mechanics)

VOCABULARY